COMMON PROBLEMS
Grownup Poetry

Double J Holste

Copyright © 2021 Double J Holste

All rights reserved. No part of this book may be reproduced or transmitted in any form or by any means, electronic or mechanical, including photocopying, recording or by any information storage and retrieval system without permission in writing from the publisher.

Jamilian Books—Harlan, IA
ISBN: 978-1-7379224-0-7
Library of Congress Control Number: 2021918726
Title: *Common Problems: Grownup Poetry*
Author: Double J Holste
Digital distribution | 2021
Paperback | 2021
This is a work of fiction. The characters, names, incidents, places, and dialogue are products of the author's imagination, and are not to be construed as real.

Dedication

This collection is dedicated to my grandmother Lilian Holste.

    For all the times we spent travelling and witnessing ridiculous humans doing ridiculous things; sharing the images we saw in the clouds with one another; spotting not one but TWO double rainbows within the same day; and for all the laughs and happiness you've provided me. **<u>I love you Gramma</u>**. Finally, as promised, here is the book I'll allow you to read. ☺

PART ONE

WHERE'S THE RELIEF?!

Fire Inside

Man,
Don't get me started,
I ate some bad chocolate last night
And shit my pants when I farted.
But what's worse,
And what really irks me the most,
Is my esophagus when I accidentally
Over-jelly my toast.
I toss and turn at night,
The burn is so unreal,
I stub my toe on the way to my Tums
And curse my last night's meal.
"Why did I have to put that Spicy Brown
On my Roast Beef?!"
I fart twice more before I finally get comfy,
But luckily they're just queefs.

Hamstring Sandwich w/ a Side of Pulled Groin

I will probably go down in history
As the World's Least Athletic Person,
Yet somehow I must move a lot
Cuz my legs and feet I'm always cursin'.
I walk up to the forklift,
spring upon it with a boing,
And with just these simple movements
Pull my hamstring AND my groin.
I started counting to myself:
"One Albuquerque, Two Albuquerque,"
But the pain was just too much
So I then gobbled like a turkey.
I don't understand this body,
I don't understand myself!
I finally get home from work
And rest my balls upon a shelf.

Toe-pit Violators

Some people call them flip-flops,
Some people call them thongs,
But when I feel those things between my toes
It's as though I'm being wronged.
My innocence is lost,
My dignity forgotten,
I walk around all day discombobulated
And downtrodden.
They set me up for failure
And I'm now forever scarred,
I lay awake at night so cold
And cry extremely hard.
By day I lock myself in my room
And hang my head in shame,
I mourn for my poor toe-pits
Cuz they'll never be the same.

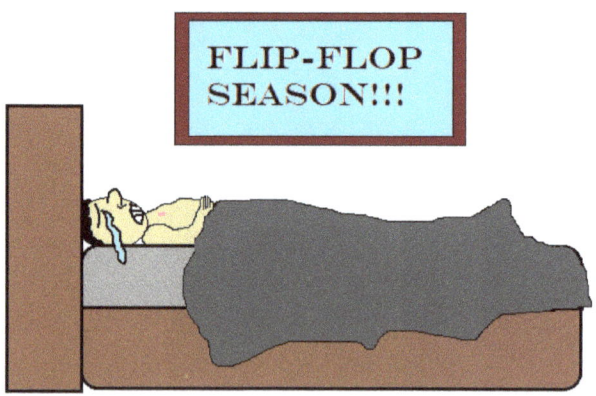

Fallen Arches

Whew!
My dogs are barkin',
I get barefoot at my house
And relish the sweet feel of my soft carpet.
There's no better way to put it
Other than I walked them off,
My arches said goodbye to me
With zero notice and a scoff.
I've never found it very funny
And now my feet are always swollen,
I tried the Gel-ish inserts
But in my shoes they both exploded.
They've kept me outta trouble
Cuz I know I'll never run,
The military refused me
And that's just fine it never sounded fun.
I have a love-hate relationship
With these assholes under my shins,
So flat they're round and ripe
Just like two bruised-up purple pumpkins…

...I have to say though,
Sometimes it's a great excuse to be a bum,
I lay around the house
And only exercise my thumb.
Dear feet, I hate and love you,
We play a complicated game,
Cuz when I get caught up being lazy
YOU will be the ones to blame.

The Unbearable Itch

I sat down the other day
Pushing hard to free my stool,
The guy in the stall next to me was laughing
And I found that less than cool.
I screamed aloud in pain,
Never had I been so plugged,
I tried to drink some Milk of Magnesia
But found an empty jug.
Finally I grabbed real tight
And nearly broke the TP holder,
Bit my upper lip and grunted:
"C'mon man be a soldier!"
I released the giant demon
In all its razor-like glory,
And I really wish that I could tell you
It was over end of story.
But there's not enough toilet paper in the world
For a job like this,
I went through half a roll
Just trying to scratch my newfound itch...

...Now I'm tired all the time
And both my hands cramp up and gripe me,
I still haven't left the stall
Cuz to this day I can't stop wiping.

PART TWO

FAMILY PROBLEMS

Meemaw's Minivan Manual

FUTURE OWNERS BEWARE:
The back doors don't shut properly
So close them with care.
This van is always beeping,
The trunk just thinks it's open,
To top it off the power steering
Screams like a pissed off locust.
And when you're pumping gas into it
The experience will make you tense,
Cuz the nozzle will shut itself off
Every 3 dollars and 32 cents.
The engine light is faulty,
Just ignore it at all costs,
I punched the dash in a heated rage,
Showing this damn thing who's boss.
This van is either haunted
Or just downright possessed,
Taking this away from me
Would also take away my stress.
And with that being said,
This is your gift and here's the key,
I'll just turn around
And you can take this piece-a-shit for FREE.

Motorcycle Mania

My brothers are the worst
Because they love to ride and brag,
They tell me I need to get one
And 'til then I'm just a drag.
They took me to the shop
And I immediately found my bike,
The Indian Scout was resting on its kickstand
Like some wild beast propped on a spike.
My brothers told me: "Take a seat!"
And my palms did get all sweaty,
I looked away and told them:
"I don't know guys, I'm not ready."
They laughed at me and called me things
That were far more than unkind,
I flushed red in embarrassment
And truly felt I'd lost my spine.
They said to try it out
if that's the one I was to get,
I ran away and cried aloud:
"I'M TOO NERVOUS FOR THIS SHIT!!!"

Grampa's Tractor

I love my goofy grampa
But sometimes he makes me nervous,
His Allis-Chalmers tractor
Is by far his favorite purchase.
He leaps onto the springy seat
Of his awesome antique tractor,
Tells me to take a few steps back
In case this thing decides to act up.
I heed his daily warning
And watch in disbelief,
Why does he love this thing so much
When all it does is give him grief?
It doesn't start right away
And he acts as if it's odd,
He smacks the steering wheel
And shouts in anger: "JESUS GOD!!!"
I tell him to try again
And by the fifth time it gets rumbling,
I say a silent prayer for him,
He does his usual mumbling.
I know what's about to happen
Cuz it has a touchy clutch,
Even with the weights up front
The takeoff is always way too much.
He lets the clutch out
And off it goes just bucking like a Bronco,
I'm hoping it doesn't throw him off
And fold him like a taco.

But he hangs on anyway,
his hat flies off with this disaster,
I look away and laugh with tears
As he drives off into the pasture.
His white hair blows and flows like mad
In the much-needed summer breeze,
And when he's done he acts as though
He did it with such ease.
He tells me it's better than John Deere
And I'm not sure if I believe him,
But his smile afterward
Is worth the troubles that precede him.

Daddy's Little Hellraiser

Dear sweet daughter of mine,
Lil' Smiley Piley,
So full of love you melt my heart
And in regard I hold you highly.
Since you were born it's been a blast,
You've been so fun to raise,
You make me so much happier
When I come home from crappy days.
I love your pretty little smile
And can't wait to show you Nintendo
But if you don't stop this crying shit,
I'm gonna throw you out the window.

The Broken-Arm Trooper

Dear son,
I always knew you were a trooper,
But you opened my eyes wider
On the night you broke your scooper.
You cried a child's cry,
Understandable and common,
You showed me your crooked arm
And in my mouth I did vomit.
We took you to the hospital
And Daddy had a buzz,
Mom was worried about your arm
And Dad was worried about the fuzz.
You wanted to make Mom feel better,
Cuz Mommy's such a crier,
You took her by the hand and said:
"At least I'm not on fire."

G-Ma's Rascal

We loaded up our G-Ma
In the Minivan toward the rear,
It was a lovely day in Branson
So we took her to the pier.
The sun was shining bright
There were no thunderclouds in sight,
And none of us were worried about
The weather of the night.
We hit up the scooter shop
And rented her a Top-of-the-Line Rascal,
For there was much walking ahead
And her knees had been a hassle.
The day had been so great,
We walked the pier 'til nearly sundown,
She wanted to leave but our argument was:
"We're having so much fun now!"
The clouds were moving in
But they were hidden by the dark,
G-Ma cruised away from us
And found a reasonable place to park.
Suddenly the rain began to plague us
With a monsoon,
The general consensus was
We better head on home soon.
As a matter of fact, you can scratch the "soon"
Because we sprinted toward the van,
I had a feeling we'd forgotten something
But my crappy feet had their own plan.
I took a look behind us
And felt like such a major asshole,

We had left her in the pouring rain
On her All-Electric Rascal.
I ran to her and scooped her up
And carried her to the van,
I felt as though she then would cry:
"Oh you strong and handsome Man!"
But as I got her in
She looked confused instead of dreamy,
She looked around at us
And said: "What the DEVIL is all that beeping?!"

Troubling Concerns in Paradise

Dear sweet wife of mine,
And by sweet I do mean salty,
I always try to help you out
But you find my actions faulty.
You make me shave my mustache
When it's quote: "Outta Control"
And my upper lip then quivers
In the Midwestern winter cold.
Now I will always love you
No matter what you've ever said,
But you're kinda the reason
I lie awake at night in bed.
I got down on one knee
And ever since it's been all chores,
Now I'm just waiting for the day
You'll ask me to get down on all fours.

PART THREE

DEEP SHIT
(THINKERS, NOT STINKERS)

My New Pet

You're helping me quit smoking
And for that I'm eternally grateful,
You've turned me into a critical thinker
And I am no longer hateful.
I take you for a walk
And then I help you go to sleep,
My favorite thing about you so far
Is you're super cheap.
I've taken you around the world
And we still haven't hit the ceiling,
This world can crush us all that way,
it's a claustrophobic feeling.
Oh my little blue Fireball,
You'll never know how much you help me,
You make me NOT wanna punch a youngin'
When I see them taking selfies.
My kids ask if they can play with you,
I tell them not to be so spastic,
"This yo-yo's High Performance, guys,
It says so on the plastic."

The Good Listener

In the wood shop by the table saws
Buzzing loudly as they cut,
I found my buddy Ted
And decided to tell him what's what.
I told him of the Bad Old Days
And how life had been so tough,
He tried to interrupt me
But I just pressed on with my stuff.
I could tell he was so interested
By the way he tilted his head,
This is my best friend, I thought,
My good ole buddy Ted.
I told him my life story
And how things had been so rotten.
Finally he said: "Dude, I can't hear you,"
And that's the best advice I'd ever gotten.

Online Grocery Shopping

My wife's the one who put the order in,
I swear she made me do it,
She even let me take the Chrysler
And told me: "There's nothing to it."
Easy Peasy, Dammit Squeezey,
I thought on my way to the store,
Found the online pick-up spot
And parked the Chrysler in stall 4.
I felt the eyes upon me
Of at least a dozen angry shoppers,
What makes this guy so special?
Is what I figured was their thought process.
There is no crappier feeling
Than when you reconsider your life choices,
I tried to justify my actions
But got bombarded by their voices.
I called the number on the sign
And told the lady where I was,
Apparently this was unacceptable
Because:
"FOUR?!"
She screamed at me through my small iPhone,
I jumped in shock and terror
And never had I felt so alone.
I repeated myself quietly
And she insisted they could make it work,
Why the hell am I doing this?
I thought and felt like such a jerk.

They got me loaded EASY PEASY,
I drove home, my thoughts conflicting,
Until later on I found out
That the lady was just practicing her golf swing.

My Dark Side

You go by Jerry Savage
Or even sometimes Juicy Susan,
When I'm with you the chances are
We'll hit the bar and start a-boozin'.
You filled me fulla darkness
And in good time the Black did fade,
But now I'm strolling in the sunshine,
There's no need for all your shade.
I gave you quite a start
And now lots of people have heard of you,
We'll let go of our past
And then I'm gonna straight-up murder you.

My Batsuit

Four bats in one year,
I've quite frankly had enough,
They sneak in through the vents I'm sure
And in my house they fly amok.
I'm certain it's the same bat
Just coming back to give me hot flash,
One of these days I'll catch him
And on his face I'll draw a mustache.
Then I'll be 100% positive
It is my same old friend,
It'll definitely make me feel better
Knowing that there isn't MORE of him.
So I'm constructing my own Batsuit,
Hence I won't be so afraid,
I'll drape myself in protective wear
And say: "C'mon Bitch, MAKE MY DAY!"
It will be a hooded sweatshirt
With a choice of my son's masks,
He'll be curious of what I'm up to
And I'll tell him: "Please don't ask."
The gloves will be that of gardening
And the net will be from the pond,
I'll keep a Sharpie in my pocket
For when I catch this Satan's spawn.
I'll hold him down and pray
That he is not a finger-tickler
And with my Sharpie draw the mustache
Which will resemble that of Hitler.

We Came, We Saw, We Got the Hell Outta There

Nomadic motel living
Was quite the priceless misadventure,
Wouldn't trade it for the world
And wouldn't try to change the picture.
I learned the minimal lifestyle,
Perhaps at an age too young,
It's definitely not something I wish
For my daughter or my son.
The world can be a scary place
And it's only growing scarier,
But as it grows, I grow, too,
My toes and knuckles harrier.
We said Goodbye to Iowa
And said Hello to freaky ghosts,
Ghosts that kept me up at night,
Yeah, they haunted me the most.
But we got the hell up outta there
And now all is well and good,
I had a lot going on upstairs
Until I stepped down from that wood.

Prank Phone Calls

There's a guy at work I like to mess with
Religiously on a daily basis,
He laughs at all my corny jokes
And overdramatic faces.
But there's something I've never told him
Cuz he just might start cussin' and yellin',
I call him every now and then
Using Star Sixty-Seven.
I put on a raspy voice
And insist that he's **The Coach**,
He just says: "Nope, you got the wrong guy,"
And I premeditate my next approach.
It's been a while since I've done this
And by now we're too busy working,
But Dear Fleabag, if you're reading this...
PLEASE FORGIVE ME AND DON'T HURT ME!!!

!!!BONUS ROUND!!!

CONGRATULATIONS!!!

You've made it to the end of my poems, don't worry, there's A LOT more where they came from. Now here's a couple gratuitous shorts to help take our minds off all those problems.
Whew!!! That was rough, right?! Just step right up and spin the wheel!
Or, turn the page, for better words...

The Porch Toad Tragedy
My High School Essay © 2007

Two weeks ago; or was it four?

I guess about a month ago, on quite a sunny morning, a jolly good friend of mine and I were getting ready to go to the State Fair. You see, Alice Cooper and Blue Oyster Cult were due to arrive the next night at the grandstand located near all the tasty treats and belchy beverages the fair had to offer.

From the basement of my companion's humble abode, we stepped outside for some fresh air and to look upon any possible damages from the storm the night before. We had heard the ruckus of thunder and suffered a thankfully short-lived power outage (I'm not embarrassed to say we snuggled close to each other in our sleep-sacks) and rejoiced in the prospect of the next day's fallen limbs. For we knew that it had rained and stormed so bad that it quite frankly stormed and rained quite much!

Because of this unorthodox August weather, many critters were bouncing about, others were squirming. Among these critters squirming and bouncing, there squatted a toad.

Since we went outside through the basement, there was a set of stairs going upwards and glass coverings on either side above, giving us the feel of standing outside of a church. We then dubbed this porch area: "The Choich."

Back to the toad. He had been squatting at the bottom of the stairway. He looked wise and he also seemed to possibly be someone's favorite uncle (can't explain it, these were my thoughts). We made eye contact for a brief period and in his eyes I found Yes, this was a decent man. An honest man, for that matter.

Probably had a wife, two kids, a solid five-year plan, and a premium policy when it comes to insurance. The toad's eyes also informed me he was very weak and weary. Life does that to people, especially when maintaining such an impressive status.

The poor toad bastard was doomed from the start.

At first, he had been squatting and not bouncing to observe his surroundings and noticed he had quite the task ahead of him. For he had to start ALL THE WAY AT THE BOTTOM of these stairs to make it to the top. *My family's up there,* is what I bet my life he was thinking.

He bounced closer to the first step, adjusted his head upwards, and made his first big leap and landed cleanly on the first stair like a champion but remained humble like a gentleman.

I'm not sure how my friend felt about this whole situation, but I was in love. I screamed aloud in joy and that's when I saw the toad turn my way and wink. I'll take that to my grave and tell my ghost friends this toad really did wink at me. All I could do was shake my head and smile. He may have been humble, but he also knew how badass he was.

That first big leap for toadkind had apparently taken a toll. I could tell by the way he kept wiping the sweat away from his eyes. Still SEVEN more stairs to go. It was going to be a long day for my new warty fellow.

But wait!

He began to hold his head high again and worked his way to the other side of the stair he had made it on, noticing it was slightly shorter due to warpage.

After giving his head another wipe, he leapt. To my dismay his little toad fingers found zero purchase and he plunged to his back on the first stair. He then decided to lay that way a while; bumpy back resting on the damp wood, yellow tummy roasting in the coming sun. I was concerned he had admitted defeat. But he rolled back over, and this time the look in his eye was murderous. My friend and I simultaneously looked away; we didn't want him taking his problems out on us. Nor did we want to offer a hand, at least not at that point. We let him keep his dignity.

And with his dignity he bounced even higher than the initial bounce, almost enough to overshoot onto the third step, and then made a landing way cooler than I have yet to see in any superhero movie. He made it to the second stair. His progress was great enough for me to almost write a letter of recommendation to my current workplace right then and there. My friend and I both applauded this time, and I was struggling with tears.

Unfortunately this endeavor had been the most taxing yet. The sweat on his brow was cascading uncontrollably. No amount of wiping could dam his tiny rivers. I could also tell he was anxious to get back to the wife, especially when he began silencing his cell phone. It was then I decided to lend a helping hand. Six more steps were six too many. And I really feel he was thinking likewise.

With utmost care and respect, I scooped him into my right hand and ignored the flow of urine in my palm. *To this poor little guy, I am a giant,* I thought. An empowering thought at that, which weeks later led me to be okay with the warts on my knuckles, but also a great learning experience to steer clear of toad piss.

I walked him to the top of the stairs and plopped him balls-first onto the cool grass of my friend's back lawn. The toad was more than grateful. Whether I gained another wink from him that day I will never know.

We were summoned inside and informed by my friend's mother that we would be waiting until the next day to leave for the fair. The weather was said to be as bad as the night before.

We awoke the next morning and again stepped outside for fresh air. As I opened the door, water came rushing over the threshold and into my socks. It had become a monsoon in "The Choich." I hopped outside quickly, and my friend followed suit, shutting the door behind us as he did so. We both jumped to the first step with the careless ease of us humans; for we were not born into the unfortunate existence of our poor toad friend. And just as I thought about all of this, I saw three little fingers poking out of the water below us.

These fingers clearly belonged to a middle-aged toad.

I reached down in a panic and brought him up from the water.

"Our little friend's a goner, I'm afraid," said my friend.

I wasn't so quick to give up hope. I laid him on the fifth step and kneeled down to give him CPR. 3 pumps, mouth-to-mouth, 3 pumps, mouth-to-mouth. I would have gone further but his mouth tasted like fly shit. At least that's what I told the ambulance when they FINALLY arrived. They were fresh out of toad body bags, so they hauled him away in my damp yet crusty sock that I had been wearing for the last two weeks (I'm a firm believer in recycling).

To this day I haven't been able to get in touch with the toad's family. My only hope is that they survived the summer's storms and are out there now frolicking in the tall grass somewhere; yellow tummies relishing the tickles.

I loved that toad. And if you just so happen to be reading this, holding the book with tiny green fingers, now mourning the loss of the father/husband/world's greatest uncle that never came back that awful day, please get in touch with me. You can easily find me on Facebook.

Old Mouse Jeff
A Gross Commemoration

In all my years of study never had I seen such a fowl sight as once I stumbled upon the ghoulish cadaver of Old Mouse Jeff.

His boiling putrescence in the mid-July climate was a mere distraction to the crusty-sock-look-alike, for his bones were well rotten and his flesh well maggot-fed.

Old Mouse Jeff had fossilized himself into my water-closet's carpet.

His appearance was that of a tiny ghost diaper.

Whence I flipped the switch and on came the warm yellow lighting of my bulbed vanity, I inspected my mis-shaven mustache with questionable concern.

How short am I to go with it? I thought, when just then I spotted behind me through the vanity mirror the very sight that haunts me even recently as I sleep.

For every night I am damned with the ruthless recollection of Old Mouse Jeff and his uncanny corpse. Which brings me to say further it was more the rapid degeneration of the poor fellow that brought on concern than just the mere thought of his demise.

I had seen him the day before, well fed he was on the corn of Sunday's banquet, spry with all the mite of a coming-of-age shithouse mouse.

We had just started calling him Old Mouse Jeff ironically, which I now realize was harshly cruel and most unnecessary. If only I had suggested we call him instead Little Big Jeff the Mouse, which was my first mindset,

I may have been spared the outlined mummy-fart on my carpet.

What, I say, what could have subdued my poor Jeff and reduced him to such hideous inexistence? If not for the corny aroma and shapely indentation, I would have assumed Old Mouse Jeff ran off to a grander landscape. A landscape un-browned by the buttcheeks of middle-class society, untainted by the sad teabags of middle-aged men, and un-fetused by the population controlling midwives of the Church Of Non-Believers whom which raid my facility without invitation.

I, sad to say, however know he's dead and not being hoisted into the various plies of life. My greatest hope is that in afterlife, Old Mouse Jeff steers clear of all future banquet corn.

And in my private quarters of unmentionable necessaries I am having the carpet removed. The old men and old women will chaff and badger me about the missing cozy texture but I for one will encourage newcomers to embrace my Brazilian life choice and treasure forever the mysterious death of my dear friend, Old Mouse Jeff.

A dark, gut-wrenching novel

Also published by Jamilian Books,
Just whip that not-so-smartphone out,
I'll thank you kindly to take a look.
For the poetry you just read
Is relative to this expanding story,
But reader be warned:
It's far much harsher and full of all that's gory.
But if that's the kinda thing you're into,
Then let me say: "YOU ARE THE BOMB!!!"
No need to Google search,
This is on Amazon.com.

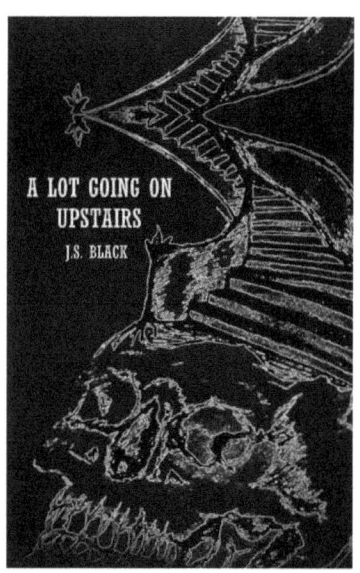

www.ingramcontent.com/pod-product-compliance
Lightning Source LLC
Chambersburg PA
CBHW040108120526
44589CB00039B/2798